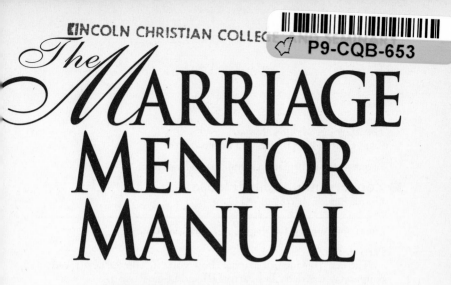

The MARRIAGE MENTOR MANUAL

How You Can Help the Newlywed Couple Stay Married

Dr. LES PARROTT III & Dr. LESLIE PARROTT

ZondervanPublishingHouse

Grand Rapids, Michigan

A Division of HarperCollins*Publishers*

The Marriage Mentor Manual
Copyright © 1995 by Les and Leslie Parrott

Requests for information should be addressed to:

■ ZondervanPublishingHouse
Grand Rapids, Michigan 49530

Library of Congress Cataloging-in-Publication Data

Parrott, Les.
    The marriage mentor manual : how you can help the newlywed couple stay married / Les Parrott III and Leslie Parrott.
        p.   cm.
    Includes bibliographical references.
    ISBN: 0-310-50131-8
    1. Marriage mentoring—United States—Handbooks, manuals, etc. 2. Marriage—United States—Handbooks, manuals, etc.   I. Parrott, Leslie, 1964–   .   II. Title.
HQ734.P215   1995
362.82'86—dc 20   95–8212
                                                                    CIP

"Still Married After Just One Year" was previously published in *Marriage Partnership* (Spring 1988) and is reprinted here by permission of Tori Carlstrom Britton.

All Scripture quotations, unless otherwise indicated, are taken from the *Holy Bible: New International Version*®. NIV®. Copyright © 1973, 1978, 1984 by International Bible Society. Used by permission of Zondervan Publishing House. All rights reserved.

Interior design by Sue Koppenol

Printed in the United States of America

99 00 01 02 /❖ DH/ 10 9 8 7 6 5

CONTENTS

96604

To Gary and Julie Collins,
a couple whose tireless energy, uncompromising integrity,
and global vision have been an inspiration
and model to us in our own marriage.

Preface

The first sentence of Chaim Potok's novel, *In the Beginning*, reads ". . . all beginnings are hard." In the book, the main character, David, describes how one evening when he was nine years old, he burst into tears because a passage of a Bible commentary had proved too difficult for him to understand. David's mentor welcomed him warmly to his apartment and spoke in a gentle voice: "Be patient, David, beginnings are hard; you cannot swallow all the world at one time."

The same is true for marriage. So often we think of a marriage ceremony as the culmination of a courtship process. But in reality, it is only a beginning. It marks the start of life-long love.

This small book is an invitation for older married couples to help newlyweds—from the beginning—build unbreakable marital bonds. By following a few of the simple guidelines in this book, and with only a minimal time commitment, you will enrich your own marriage and become a lasting blessing to a couple during their first year of married life together.

Perhaps you are already mentoring a young couple. This book will help you hone your skills. Or maybe you are just considering how you might be a positive influence in the life of a newly married couple. This book can be your guide. It is a user's manual—brief and to the point. It is meant to provide you with a practical plan and give you the essential skills for helping newlyweds get started on the right foot. You won't find bulky explanations or heavy theory, just straightforward how-to's.

While you may read *The Marriage Mentor Manual* on your own, it is also designed to be used in conjunction with the *Saving Your Marriage Before It Starts* (SYMBIS) curriculum kit. In brief, the SYMBIS kit includes: (1) a book for newlyweds that focuses on seven questions to ask before and after getting married; (2) a workbook for men and a workbook for women; (3) an eight-session video package; and (4) a leader's guide. This kit can be used to set up a comprehensive marriage preparation program that includes a marriage mentorship program. Appendix B, "Setting Up a Mentoring Program," describes this program in more detail.

Whether you are using this manual on your own or in conjunction with the SYMBIS program, it will help you pass on to other couples what God has given to you. It is assumed that if you are using this book, you and your partner have been happily married a number of years. Of course, no marriage is perfect, but being an effective mentor couple does not require perfection. It simply asks that you be who you are.

Down through the centuries, young people have learned most through careful observation of those who are more experienced. As a mentor couple you offer young newlyweds the same opportunity. In subtle and not so subtle ways, you will model inspiring qualities and communicate those qualities to a couple entering the passage of their first married year.

We cannot thank you enough for allowing a newly married couple to peer into your lives and learn from your time-tested relationship. We know you are sacrificing much to give yourselves to these "novices," but we know you will be doubly blessed in return.

Les and Leslie Parrot
Center for Relationship Development
Seattle Pacific University
Seattle, Washington

> We loved you so much that we were delighted to share with you not only the gospel of God but our lives as well.
>
> 1 THESSALONIANS 2:8

CHAPTER ONE:

THE FINE ART OF MARRIAGE MENTORING

Tom and Wendy were the typical newly married couple. In their mid-twenties, they had dated for nearly two years before getting engaged. They had the blessing of their parents, attended premarital counseling, and were on their way to living happily ever after—or so everyone thought.

But marriage for Tom and Wendy, like the majority of newlyweds, wasn't all they hoped for. Each of them, for different reasons, felt a bit slighted. Unlike the majority of couples, however, Tom and Wendy talked openly about their feelings. The expectations they had of marriage were not getting met, and they were determined to do something about it. So on a cold January day, eight months after their wedding, Tom and Wendy asked for help.

Bundled up against the cold, they came into our office and began to shed their coats. As Wendy sipped hot coffee to thaw out, she said: "We have talked to friends and family about what is going on, but we both decided we needed more objectivity."

Tom joined in: "Yeah, everybody who knows us just says 'give it time' or something like that." Tom went on to say that their marriage was not suffering a major trauma, no major overhaul was needed, only, as he said, "a little realignment."

We met with Tom and Wendy for nearly an hour, listening to their experiences. We gave them a couple of exercises to help them explore their misconceptions of marriage, and we recommended a few resources. Then we talked about the idea of linking up with a marriage mentor couple.

"What's that?" they both asked.

We told them how meeting from time to time with a married couple could give them a sounding board and a safe place to explore some of their questions about marriage. Like most newly married couples we talk to, Tom and Wendy were very eager to find such a couple. After a bit of discussion, they suggested a married couple in their church. Neither of them knew the couple very well, but they respected their marriage from afar and thought they would fit the bill. After a couple of phone calls and a little more exploration, we made the connection for Tom and Wendy. Over the course of several months, they met three times with their mentors, Nate and Sharon.

Tom and Wendy have been married more than five years now. They are not the perfect couple, but they are madly in love and happier than they ever imagined. Here is a portion of a letter they recently wrote to us:

Dear Les and Leslie,

How can we ever thank you for helping us find a marriage mentor couple? Before coming to you we had never even heard of such an idea. But needless to say, our mentoring relationship with Nate and Sharon ended up being the most important thing we have ever done to build up our marriage. It was so nice to have another couple know what we were going through and remain objective at the same time.

We have since moved to another state, but on our wedding anniversary, Nate and Sharon always give us a call to celebrate our marriage.

Anyway, we are writing to say thank you and to say that you should tell more people about the benefits of marriage mentoring. Someday we hope to give back the gift that Nate and Sharon gave to us by mentoring some newly married couples. We think every couple just starting out should have a mentor.

That's not a bad idea. Marriage mentoring is one of the most significant helps to building a life-long marriage we know of. We have seen hundreds of couples strengthen their new marriages through mentoring relationships and have known the difference it can make. It really is time we take the time-honored tool of mentoring and apply it to marriage.

TODAY'S NEED FOR MENTORS

Throughout human history, mentoring has been the primary means of passing on knowledge and skills in every field and in every culture. In the past, mentoring took place in the university, where a student learned under the supervision of a scholar. It took place in the studio, where the artist poured himself into the formation of his protégés. The Bible is certainly filled with examples of mentoring (Eli and Samuel, Elijah and Elisha, Moses and Joshua, Naomi and Ruth, Elizabeth and Mary, Barnabas and Paul, Paul and Timothy). Up until recently, mentoring was a way of life between the generations. But today, mentoring is in short supply.

Mentoring was once assumed, expected, and therefore, almost unnoticed because of its commonness. But in the modern age, the learning process has shifted. It now relies primarily on computers, classrooms, books, and videos. In most cases today, the relational connection between the knowledge-and-experience giver and the receiver has weakened or is nonexistent.

The time has come to bring back the fine art of mentoring.

WHAT IS A MENTOR?

Does the near disappearance of mentoring mean it is no longer helpful? Absolutely not. Ask any successful leader and he or she will tell you: A young person starting out in a career, for example, will benefit greatly from having a mentor—an older, experienced person who knows the ropes and will teach a protégé how things are done.

The term *mentor* arises from an unlikely source. It first appeared in Greek mythology when Ulysses asked a wise man named Mentor, in Homer's *Odyssey*, to care for his son, Telemachus, while Ulysses was fighting in the Trojan War. Mentor taught the boy "not only in book learning but also in the wiles of the world." The fabled Mentor must have done his job well, because Telemachus grew up to be an enterprising lad who gallantly helped his father recover his kingdom.

But mentoring is more than the stuff of legends. A real-life mentor, one who serves as a model and provides individualized help and encouragement, can be invaluable to a receptive mentoree. The following list summarizes some of the most important roles a mentor plays:

- Mentors give timely information to mentorees.
- Mentors model various aspects of what they wish to impart.
- Mentors challenge and motivate mentorees to move to higher levels.
- Mentors direct mentorees to helpful resources when needed.
- Mentors encourage goodness and inspire greatness.
- Mentors lessen mentorees' anxiety by normalizing experiences.
- Mentors help mentorees set goals.
- Mentors keep mentorees accountable to their goals.
- Mentors provide a periodic review and evaluation of mentorees' performance.

A word of caution is in order: Mentors can do all of the things mentioned above and still not be effective. Two dynamics are vital to the success of any mentoring relationship. Without them, all the modeling, challenging, encouraging, goal setting, accountability, and so on, will fall flat. The two critical dynamics are *attraction* and *responsiveness*.

Attraction is the starting point in every effective mentoring relationship. The mentor and the mentoree must be drawn to each other to some degree. If either side is not genuinely interested in the other, true mentoring will never take place. Along with this attractiveness, the mentoree must be willing and ready to learn from the mentor. Without a responsive attitude and a receptive spirit on the part of the mentoree, little genuine mentoring can occur.

WHAT IS A MARRIAGE MENTOR?

Through our Center for Relationship Development at Seattle Pacific University we have helped coordinate hundreds of marriage mentoring relationships and know firsthand how beneficial this relationship can be. While not every couple who comes through our programming chooses to participate in the mentoring program, the majority do. And after years of following these relationships we have come to believe that there is no single way to be a marriage mentor.

We define a marriage mentor as *a happy, more experienced couple who empowers a newly married couple through sharing resources and relational experiences.*

It is a broad definition because there is no one right way to mentor. Each mentoring relationship takes on its own style and personality. The amount of time couples spend together and the content they discuss can rarely be prescribed. However, after years of working with many mentoring couples, we recommend a minimum of three meetings throughout the newlyweds' first year together:

1. at three months after the wedding
2. at seven months after the wedding
3. at twelve months after the wedding

Later in this book we discuss these three meeting times in depth and give you suggestions for taking advantage of their unique developmental phases. Marriage mentoring, however, is by no means limited to these three meetings. You may find that additional meetings are helpful, or perhaps scheduled phone contacts, and so on. We have also seen the effectiveness of an additional separate meeting or two between the males from each partner and the females from each partner. These one-on-one times allow each partner to discuss issues that they may not feel comfortable discussing together.

While every marriage mentoring relationship has its own style that unfolds as the relationship develops, some potential confusion can be spared if the mentors and mentorees discuss their initial expectations of the relationship. This discussion, of course, necessitates the mentoring couple to be clear on their "style" before meeting with the mentorees. For example, you may want to discuss whether you see yourselves more as models or as coaches, more as teachers or as guides, and so on. What is it that you want to bring to the mentoring relationship?

What a Mentor Is Not

"What I need is someone to talk to who has walked down the path I'm just beginning," said Lisa, four months into her new marriage. "Whenever I go to my mom or dad with a situation they end up parenting me or teaching me something I don't really need to learn."

Lisa, like most newlyweds we have met, needs a mentor. Mom and Dad certainly serve a helpful function in the life of a new bride or groom, but they cannot usually offer the distance and objectivity that a mentor gives. For this reason, it is important to realize exactly what a mentor is not. The following is a list of mentoring pitfalls we have witnessed. We offer it as a guide to keeping you from making the same mistakes:

- A mentor is not a mother or father.
- A mentor is not automatically a pal or a buddy.
- A mentor is not "on call" for every little crisis. His or her time is limited to discussion about major situations, not minor ones.
- A mentor is not committed long-term. The association has a natural cycle of its own, not always predictable.
- A mentor is not a teacher.
- A mentor is not a know-it-all.

A mentor is *a happy, more experienced couple who empowers a newly married couple through sharing resources and relational experiences.* Keeping this definition in mind can help you avoid costly mistakes and help your mentorees start off on the right foot.

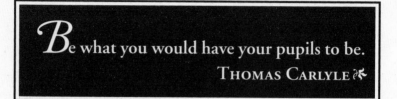

CHAPTER TWO:

ARE YOU FIT TO BE A MARRIAGE MENTOR?

Brian was a bright, articulate person. He and Sarah had been married more than a decade. They had their ups and downs, but for the most part they were happy together. From all appearances, Brian and Sarah had what it takes to be effective marriage mentors—except for one thing. Brian had a habit of making snap judgments. As Sarah sometimes said, Brian was trigger happy with advice. While this trait was certainly helpful at times, it did not serve him well as a mentor. He came across as task oriented and impatient.

Lisa was extremely compassionate. She was known for being sensitive to the needs of others and for always being

ARE YOU FIT TO BE A MARRIAGE MENTOR?

willing to lend a helping hand. Lisa and her husband, Ryan, seemed to be good candidates for being marriage mentors, but Lisa's greatest strength was also a weakness that had potential to undermine a mentoring relationship. Lisa could not stand conflict of any kind and avoided it at all costs. She liked to gloss over trouble spots and paint everything with happiness. She discounted disagreements and saw everything as being great.

The single most important factor in effective marriage mentoring is who you are as a couple. Regardless of your education, training, or natural relational skills, if certain qualities are not brought to the mentoring relationship, there will be little chance of it being successful. The following self-inventory can help determine the degree to which you possess some of these traits.

MARRIAGE MENTORING SELF-TEST

For each statement below, indicate the response that best identifies your beliefs and attitudes. Keep in mind that the "right" answer is the one that best expresses your thoughts at this time. Use the following code:

5 = I strongly agree
4 = agree
3 = I am undecided
2 = I disagree
1 = I strongly disagree

——— 1. Giving advice has little to do with good mentoring.

——— 2. I can accept and respect people who disagree with me.

——— 3. I can make a mistake and admit it.

——— 4. I look at everybody's side of a disagreement before I make a decision.

——— 5. I tend to trust my intuition even when I'm unsure of the outcome.

——— 6. I don't need to see immediate and concrete results in order to know progress is occurring.

——— 7. Who you are in mentoring is more important than what you do.

——— 8. My presence frees others from the threat of external evaluation.

——— 9. In a tense emotional situation I tend to remain calm.

——— 10. I know my limits when it comes to helping others.

——— *Total Score*

Total your responses to determine the degree to which you have the qualities necessary to be an effective mentor:

40–50   You are well on your way to being an effective mentor; take special care to maintain the qualities you have.

ARE YOU FIT TO BE A MARRIAGE MENTOR?

30–39   You have what it takes to be effective, but
         you will need to exert special attention to
         groom the traits described in this chapter.
below 30 Seek out another's advice and counsel to
         assess your strengths more accurately.

THE EFFECTIVE MENTOR

Many researchers have attempted to identify the qualities that make up the successful mentor: sensitivity, hope, compassion, awareness, knowledge . . . the list could fill several pages. However, when all of the traits are taken into account, three emerge as essential: warmth, genuineness, and empathy.

Warmth

Everyone knows what it feels like to be with someone who is warm. Mentors who possess warmth bring a sense of relaxation and comfort to the relationship. They have an attitude that does not evaluate or require change. In short, they accept their mentoree. It's not that mentors approve of everything their mentorees do; mentors simply accepts their mentorees—maybe in spite of things they do not necessarily like. Warmth is not a kind of smothering sentimentality; it simply allows mentors to respect mentorees and treat them as worthy people. Warmth frees mentorees from the need to win approval.

Without a generous supply of warmth, some mentoree couples will perform in order to get approval and win their mentors' acceptance.

Genuineness

All of us have a built-in radar that spots phoniness. We are experts at detecting fabricated feelings and insincere intentions. We apply our own private polygraph test to every human interaction. That is why it is essential that mentors be genuine. Genuineness cannot be faked. Either you sincerely want to help, or you are simply playing the sterile role of a "mentor"—hiding behind masks, defenses, or facades. In other words, authenticity is something you *are*, not something you *do*. Genuineness has been described as a lure to the heart. Jesus said, "Blessed are the pure in heart." Or, to put it another way, "Consider the mentor in whom there is no guile." When genuineness is present, a hesitant and even skeptical couple is likely to stay with you and invest energy in the mentoring process.

Empathy

The best way to avoid stepping on the toes of the couple you are mentoring is to put yourself in their shoes. Empathy lets them know you hear their words, understand their thoughts, and sense their feelings. This does not mean you necessarily understand all that is going on for them. It means you understand what they feel and think. Empathy is more than feeling their feelings; it is also being objective enough to not allow your feelings to blend with theirs.

> *P*eople are not very good at taking orders, but they are great at imitating.
> WAYMAN MITCHELL

CHAPTER THREE:

THE HEART OF EFFECTIVE MARRIAGE MENTORING

When we approach some people about being marriage mentors they often say, "We don't know how to mentor." Or they tell us that their marriage isn't all it could be. We have heard dozens of seemingly good reasons for not being mentors to newly married couples, but we have also discovered that very few of them hold up.

You don't have to be marriage "experts" to be effective marriage mentors. Just being aware of the challenges that face any new husband and wife can place you in a position to listen, ask helpful questions, and be an encourager. You don't need to know "all the answers" to be an effective marriage mentor. In this chapter we give you the basic tools for mentoring, and they are all wrapped up in a single word: listening.

Active listening—listening with "the third ear" as Theodor Reik called it—is the heart of effective marriage mentoring.

Jesus understood the importance of listening. Even as a young boy he was sitting with the teachers in the temple, "listening to them and asking them questions [and] everyone was amazed at his understanding" (Luke 2:46). The Apostle Paul understood that listening requires diligent work. When he was before Agrippa, he said, "I beg you to listen to me patiently" (Acts 26:3). The book of James tells us to "be quick to listen and slow to speak" (1:19). And the book of Proverbs says: "If one gives answer before he hears, it is his folly and shame" (18:13). The word *listen* occurs over two hundred times in the Bible.

There are two major ingredients that go into active listening: reflection and clarification.

ACTIVE LISTENING REQUIRES REFLECTION AND CLARIFICATION

Understanding comes through empathic reflection—responding sensitively to the emotional, rather than the semantic meaning, of a person's expression. Many believe that sincerity assures understanding. But sincerity ignores the fact that we communicate in ways that severely limit our ability to get our real messages across. A mentor can have all the sincerity in the world, but without the tool of reflective listening, little good can be done.

Between what a person intends to communicate and what others hear stands an unavoidable filter of pre-conception. "I'm not going to do another goofy exercise" may mean, "I am too embarrassed to tell you that I feel inadequate." "I can't let go of the checkbook" may mean, "I don't want to let go of controlling our finances." Or, "Do you really think so?" may mean, "I disagree."

A mentor can target three aspects of a message in making a reflective statement: (1) the content of the message, (2) the thinking behind the message, and (3) the feeling behind the message. Each is equally valid and useful. Here is an example of how a single statement may be reflected at each level.

New Wife:	I couldn't believe he was accusing me for what *he* did.
Mentor Reflecting Content:	He blamed you.
New Wife:	Yeah. He said I was the one responsible because I was there.
Mentor Reflecting Thinking:	You thought he was unfair.
New Wife:	Yeah. I didn't deserve to be blamed.
Mentor Reflecting Feeling:	It must have made you angry.
New Wife:	I was furious. I also felt bad.

By reflecting the content of the message, the mentor allows the mentoree to elaborate further on what happened. By reflecting the thinking behind the message, the mentor allows mentorees to understand their evaluation of what happened. And by reflecting the feeling behind the message, mentorees are invited to become aware of the emotions they are feeling as a result of what happened.

While each of these areas of reflection is important, focusing on feelings is perhaps the most important aspect of reflection for mentors. Here are a few more examples:

New Husband: I didn't know how she would respond to my wanting her to take more responsibility for the budget, but she was very eager to do it.

Mentor Reflecting Feeling: You must be happy.

New Husband: I was really relieved. It feels great.

New Wife: We thought setting up our home would be fun, but it turned into a minor disaster when we couldn't agree on where to place a single picture.

Mentor Reflecting Feeling: Sounds frustrating.

New Wife: It was. But we got over it and finally got our act together.

By reflecting the feelings of a newlywed, we are not evaluating or advising. We are saying, "I am with you and want to understand you better." Reflecting feelings may not seem like much to offer, but it is more than a newly married couple will get from anyone else. And it is far better than offering advice.

AN EXERCISE IN ACTIVE LISTENING

Important feelings are often hidden behind the words of a newlywed. Reflecting his or her feelings is one of the most helpful and difficult listening techniques to implement. Following are some typical newlywed statements. Read each separately, listening for feelings. Make note of the feeling you hear and write out a response that reflects that feeling for each of the statements.

1. We work at communication skills all the time, but it doesn't make any difference.

    _____

    _____

2. Every other couple seemed to get an invitation but us.

    _____

    _____

3. I shouldn't have slammed the door, but she shouldn't have said that.

    _____

    _____

4. I should be able to go wherever I want. He does.

    _____

    _____

5. Do you think I did the right thing?

    _____

    _____

6. Sometimes I feel myself biting my tongue
   when I'd really like to tell him how upset I am.

    _____

    _____

7. I don't want to talk about it anymore.

    _____

    _____

    _____

8. If we aren't getting anywhere on an issue, I just
   need to take a time-out. I mean, what's the use?

    _____

    _____

9. Sometimes I feel like I am living out a fairy tale.
   I never dreamed marriage would be so great.

    _____

    _____

10. I don't feel anything about it.

    _____

    _____

Now compare your list of reflective statements to those listed at the end of the chapter to see how accurately you recognize feelings. Give yourself a 2 on those items where your choice closely matches, a 1 on items where your choice only partially matches, and a 0 if you missed altogether.

How you rate on recognizing feelings:

16–20 Above average recognition of feelings.

11–15 Average recognition of feelings.

0–10   Below average recognition of feelings.

What Active Listening Does

Listening unearths hidden feelings.

Active listing allows a person's hidden feelings to percolate to the top. Newlyweds do not often broadcast their pain. They want someone to sense their hurt without their having to admit it. Their anxiety about a particular circumstance, for example, sometimes hides behind a smiling face.

To help newlyweds, you need a sensitive, internal seismograph to feel the subterranean tremors underneath the external calm. In effect, that is what active listening is—a way to sense the inevitable quakings of a new marriage. If you have a hunch that a bride is not as apathetic as she seems, but actually angry because her husband isn't as sensitive as she once thought, don't blurt out: "You are denying how angry you really are." Instead you may probe gently: "Something about the way you're talking gives me the sense that you might be angry but feel you're not supposed to be." A statement like this allows a newlywed to own her buried disappointment without losing face.

Listening takes away the fear of emotions.

Free from evaluation, active listening creates a safe environment. It provides a place where a trembling newlywed can shed defenses and own up to previously feared emotions. It allows them to say their feelings are acceptable. When newlyweds are guarded, it is as if they are holding the accelerator all the way down but keeping the car in neutral and their foot on the brake—using valuable fuel and going nowhere. Active listening can give a young partnership new energy and help them begin to move in a positive direction.

Listening helps newlyweds mature.

The marriage mentor's goal is to not be depended upon. Mentoring isn't rescuing. Too often we mistake help with throwing out a line of advice. The problem with solving a couple's problems is that external solutions foster unhealthy dependence. If you solve a problem for a new couple who comes back repeatedly with a similar problem the next month, you are putting out the same fire over and over. When we listen to newlyweds, we are, in effect, saying, "I believe in you and your marriage." But giving advice says, "I don't trust you to come up with your own solution." Active listening boosts the confidence of newlyweds and teaches them to depend on God and themselves for problem solving.

Useful Leads for the Active Listener	
It sounds like you're feeling . . .	It seems as if . . .
I get a picture of . . .	What I hear you saying is . . .
Could it be that . . .	It must have been . . .
I'm wondering if you're thinking . . .	You must feel . . .

WHY ADVICE CAN TURN SOUR

Too often, advice cuts the heart out of effective mentoring. A little advice, like a little garlic, goes a long way. The following reminders may help you keep from overdoing it.

Advice is often self-centered.

When we dole out advice that is not cushioned with active listening, we often believe we are being helpful. But an attempt to help a couple by giving advice is not only naive and ineffective but often self-serving. It hurts to see a new couple struggle, so by doing our part—bestowing advice—we feel better. The driving motive behind eager advice is often a desire to feel good about yourself.

Advice can make a couple feel worse.

Offering advice can set a couple up to feel worse because they cannot or are not ready to follow through on it. This can instill terrible pangs of guilt. The advice that Job's friends gave him in his time of affliction, for example, only served to make poor Job more miserable. The only way a mentor can know when and if a couple is ready for advice is through persistent and sensitive listening.

Advice can be threatening.

Sometimes giving advice can call another person's beliefs and attitudes into question. When this occurs it is most likely advice that is being given out of our insecurity concerning our own personal beliefs. It is uncomfortable for us to be uncertain of our own values on certain issues. So, we reason, if we convert a new couple to our way of thinking, it would not only relieve our discomfort, it would be further proof of the validity of our beliefs, and it would cast us into the role of an all-knowing mentor to boot.

Advice can be boring.

Being forced to sit through an unrewarding or even irritating monologue causes people to turn off the one-way conversation and put their minds on something else. Bored listeners simply suppress their impulse to walk out by taking a mental vacation and sitting it out. Without self-restraint, the bored couple would be like the young child who was bored in church, looked up at his mom, and said, "Pay the man and let's go home." Advice given without active listening causes boredom. And as Proverbs says, "he who answers before listening—that is his folly and his shame" (18:13).

The point is plain. It is difficult to make a mistake with active listening.

Possible Responses to the Exercise in Active Listening

1. We work at communication skills all the time, but it doesn't make any difference.—Sounds like you feel discouraged.

2. Every other couple seemed to get an invitation but us.—It feels kind of like you got left out?

3. I shouldn't have slammed the door, but she shouldn't have said that.—You feel kind of guilty, but at the same time, justified for what you did.

4. I should be able to go wherever I want. He does.—I wonder if you feel like your partner is being overly protective.

5. Do you think I did the right thing?—It sounds like you're not real sure of yourself.

6. Sometimes I feel myself biting my tongue when I'd really like to tell him how upset I am.—You feel really angry at times.

7. I don't want to talk about it anymore.—It sounds as if you're feeling overloaded, like it is all just too much.

8. If we aren't getting anywhere on an issue, I just need to take a time-out. I mean, what's the use?—As you say that I get a picture of a guy who is discouraged and is crying uncle.

9. Sometimes I feel like I am living out a fairy tale. I never dreamed marriage would be so great.—Sounds like you couldn't feel happier.

10. I don't feel anything about it.—I'm wondering if you have some idea of what you should be feeling and because you are not feeling that way, you register it as not feeling anything.

> *H*e who chooses the beginning of a road
> chooses the place it leads to.
> HARRY EMERSON FOSDICK

CHAPTER FOUR:

THE THIRD-MONTH MEETING: MAKING CONTACT

A recent newspaper account told of a young wife who was at first frantic and later incensed because her husband did not come home from work one evening. They had returned from their honeymoon, and after his first day back at the office the young husband drove to his parents' suburban home instead of to his own apartment. The new husband simply forgot he was married.

Stories like that are rare, but it is easy to understand this absent-minded husband's faux pas. The first few months of marriage require a tremendous amount of adjusting and readjusting. For some couples this time is characterized by an elongated honeymoon phase, but for many others, it is one of the most difficult times of their marriage.

Think back to the first three months of your marriage. What fears did you encounter? How were your expectations altered? How did you handle your conflicts? We recommend that you take a moment to discuss with your partner the first three months of your marriage. Try to recall as many details as you can—the good and the bad—and focus on the emotions that were a part of that time.

Recalling your early months of marriage will help you better empathize with the couples you mentor. By putting yourselves in their shoes, you will more quickly identify with their world and facilitate a healthy bond.

THE THIRD MONTH OF MARRIAGE

While not every couple encounters the same issues during their first three months, there are some areas that are quite predictable: setting up a new home, agreeing on financial management, and negotiating marital roles.

Setting Up a New Home

Trying to establish a new home together is a major challenge. In *Saving Your Marriage Before It Starts*, we describe a couple who couldn't even agree on where to hang a single picture. We have known other couples who divvied out rooms, his and hers, that would be decorated to their individual tastes. While these are extreme examples, the tension that underlies the task of making a home one's own is difficult to exaggerate. So when you mentor a couple during this period, remember that this seemingly elementary task can be the cause of much angst.

Agreeing on Financial Management

Money. That single word is surrounded by more power, more emotion, more symbolism, and more myth than almost any other word in the English language. It evokes a jumble of responses: envy, joy, fear, guilt, lust, hope, scorn. And when two people are intimately involved with money—as in marriage—the dynamics can become explosive. Money is the leading cause of marital difficulty, and we don't like to talk about it. And many newlyweds avoid talking about it like the plague.

Negotiating Marital Roles

Who takes out the trash? Who fills the car with gas? Who makes the bed? Every little daily chore in a new marriage needs to be negotiated. Each marriage partner brings his or her own private expectation of how the nitty-gritty parts of marriage are supposed to work. They have each observed models in their own parents and have either absorbed their respective roles or rebelled against them. Either way, every three-month-old marriage is going to be faced with the process of negotiating how each person is going to behave in their relationship.

MAKING CONTACT

The very first contact you have with your mentoree couple may occur over the phone, by letter, or in person. But regardless of the means, the message should be clear: *We are thrilled to walk with you through your first year.* Excitement should not be in short supply. Newlyweds need to know you are overjoyed about their new life together and that you are honored to be a part of it. In other words, your first contact should express a sense of eager anticipation.

The pragmatic goal of the first contact is to set a time for the four of you to get together. It is important to make specific arrangements for meeting sometime during their third or fourth month of marriage. While it is great to invite them into your home for a meal or a snack, it may be more simple to meet at a restaurant for a cup of coffee. The goal it not to entertain, but to mentor.

WHAT TO TALK ABOUT

This three-month meeting is more a time of getting acquainted than anything else. Of course, how this occurs depends a great deal on your personalities. Some couples need very little structure to do this, while others may need to be probed a bit more. At any rate, don't hesitate to reveal who you are. Talk about how you met and what you enjoy about marriage. But don't forget that the main focus should be on your mentorees. Ask them how they met, how long they dated, how they got engaged, what their wedding was like—all the while practicing the active listening skills described in chapter 3.

In addition to getting to know your mentorees, this first session should also focus on the couple's personal goals for marriage. What kind of marriage do they want to build? What marriages have they seen that they respect? What qualities, patterns, behaviors, and rituals do they want to incorporate in their marriage?

In exploring their goals for marriage, you may want to use the "Achieving a Shared Vision Sheet" located on the following page. The Shared Vision sheet is designed to help newlyweds forge a vision/goal statement for their marriage. We suggest that you copy it and send it to them before getting together. This will help the mentoree couple prepare for your time together and give you some concrete information to explore.

During the first meeting, you will also want to take advantage of an excellent resource, *Marriage Partnership* magazine. We have used this magazine in marriage mentoring for years and find it invaluable. This quarterly magazine provides a common jumping-off point for discussing a number of topics. For example, once both of you are receiving the magazine, you may ask your mentorees what grabbed their attention in the last issue. This question will allow them to bring up any topic that is important to them.

Achieving a Shared Vision

One of the most important, yet least talked about issues of marriage is the vision you share for your relationship. Take a moment to discuss what you hope to achieve (i.e., your goals) as a couple. What would you like to accomplish at three months, at seven months, and at one year? Consider communication and conflict, spirituality, intimacy, financial management, outside relationships, traditions for holidays, and so on. Be as specific as possible.

Our goals at three months:

_____

_____

_____

_____

Our goals at seven months:

_____

_____

_____

_____

Our goals at one year:

_____

_____

_____

_____

What are some of the roadblocks that could prevent you from meeting these goals?

_____

_____

_____

_____

Also, during your first meeting you should set up the kind of relationship you want to have during your year together. For example, would it be okay for them to call you? What about contacting them from time to time by phone? and so on.

Before concluding your first meeting you will want to talk about and schedule your next time together. It is important to have a specific date on the calendar that they can look forward to and count on.

One final note about this first meeting: We have discovered that mentoree couples sometimes invite their mentor couple over for a meal at some point. If this happens, by all means, accept their invitation. Do not play it down. Having you into their new home can be an important step in helping them form a marriage identity. And affirming their hospitality is a great way of solidifying the mentoring relationship.

A QUICK REVIEW LIST FOR THE FIRST MENTOR MEETING

You may find it helpful to review the following suggestions before your first session:

- Remember that a mentor is not a marriage counselor. You are simply to become healthy models of support for your couple.
- Celebrate the excitement of the couple's new beginning (remember your first year?).

- Inspire your couple by letting them know that marriage *is* great!
- Let the couple know that struggles are a normal part of marriage and that it is best to talk about them.
- Use your own true life-stories as a point of encouragement.
- Be vulnerable when appropriate (e.g., letting them know your own struggles).
- Try not to foster dependency upon you. The true mentor has no disciples.
- Be open to learning how you can learn from your newly married couple.
- Stay away from giving advice. Like garlic, a little goes a long way.
- Empathize with your couple by putting yourself in their shoes.
- Listen, listen, listen.

NOTE: If you are part of a sponsored marriage mentoring team, do not forget to complete the Meeting Response Form (in appendix C of this book) and send it to your marriage mentor coordinator.

> *M*entoring is a brain to pick, a shoulder to cry on, and a kick in the pants.
>
> JOHN C. CROSBY

CHAPTER FIVE:

THE SEVENTH-MONTH MEETING: STRENGTHENING THE BOND

Todd and Linda couldn't believe they had been married more than half of a year. "It has gone so quickly," said Linda. "It feels like we got married just a few days ago." But Todd and Linda had come through a critical passage that signified they were not still on their honeymoon—they had run into their first big fight. Neither remembers what it was really about, but they feel good about getting through it and are optimistic about the strength of their relationship. They have overcome a few hurdles, know there are still more down the road, and are up for the challenge.

By the seventh month of marriage most couples, like Todd and Linda, have encountered a strong dose of reality. They have clashed openly and are realizing that marriage doesn't just happen, that it takes work.

Stewart and Terri, also married about seven months, had certainly come to realize the difficulties of marriage. While still very committed, they were not quite as optimistic as Todd and Linda. Both expected marriage to be more than what it was. They had not encountered any huge disappointments or surprises by their seventh month, but each of them felt that there must be more. They were a little disillusioned by marriage as a whole and were in desperate need of support and encouragement.

Todd and Linda, happy and eager, and Stewart and Terri, disillusioned and persevering, were in the same stage of marriage but at different places. But both were primed to receive the benefits of marriage mentoring. By the seventh month, couples have come to a place where the real work of mentoring begins.

THE SEVENTH MONTH OF MARRIAGE

While not every couple encounters the same issues during their first seven months, there are some areas that are quite predictable: managing conflict, dealing with in-law relations, and preparing for holidays.

Managing Conflict

Most newlyweds will have encountered their first major blow-up before their seventh month of marriage.

By this time they have most likely fallen into some potentially destructive patterns of fighting that can be remedied if they learn the most effective ways of managing conflict. Fighting a good fight is not easy. In truth it often takes years to master, but newlyweds at this stage will certainly be eager students to know how to minimize their times of tension.

Dealing with In-Law Relations

At about seven months, most couples have stirred up a lot of feelings about their families. Trying to sort out what kind of relationship to have with one's own family and a spouse's family can be a challenge. But resolving this issue is vital to the health of a marriage. The goal for newlyweds, of course, is to shift allegiances away from family and friends and focus their allegiances on each other. This is not always easy for couples, especially after only seven months of marriage—but it is none too soon to make the shift.

Preparing for Holidays

Celebrating holidays is extremely important to a new marriage. How a couple celebrates Thanksgiving, Christmas, the New Year, and so on, during their first year together often sets a pattern for all the holidays that follow. Typically, these holidays have been spent with their families, and they never had to blend new and different traditions into their own. And too often, newly-weds do not deliberately consider how to prepare for holidays as a couple. The holidays can become a source of tremendous stress and lead to unnecessary conflict. But by thinking their arrangements through and planning ahead, couples can set up positive patterns that forever enrich their relationship.

WHAT TO TALK ABOUT

In this second session, it is important to wrap up any loose ends from your last meeting. Often, a statement or even an off-the-cuff remark may have been lodged in your mentorees' minds and, after several months, they may now be ready to better hear something that was brought up in your last session. So begin by reviewing your last time together. What thoughts or comments do they have about it?

After clearing up any old business, you may then want to touch on the seven-month goals they noted in their Achieving a Shared Vision Sheet. You may also want to explore the highlights of their new marriage. What are they enjoying most about marriage? What pleasant surprises have they discovered? This can lead nicely into a brief discussion about any trouble spots they have encountered. What has been their biggest challenge thus far? At this point, the couple may bring up the issue of conflict, in-laws, holidays, or any number of things. Your job, just to remind you, is not necessarily to solve their problem or offer solutions, but simply to listen, accurately understanding and empathizing with their struggles. This kind of empathy will help them open up even more and eventually come to terms with their struggles on their own.

Another item of discussion could be any topic from your most recent issue of *Marriage Partnership* magazine. Ask them what they read and what they found helpful.

Because the issue of in-laws is so critical to this stage of marriage, you may want to bring this issue up explicitly, if your mentorees don't. A starting point may be to reminisce about how you and your partner experienced in-law situations during your first year. Or an open-ended question about how each of your mentorees is feeling about relating to both families is often enough to do the trick. However, you may also want to use the following inventory as a springboard for generating a more open discussion on the topic.

A QUICK REVIEW LIST FOR THE SECOND MENTOR MEETING

You may find it helpful to review the following suggestions before your second session:

- Keep in mind that you are not a marriage counselor. You are a supportive model.
- Affirm and encourage the couple's progress.

The In-Law Inventory

Place a check next to each of the statements that apply to you.

In relating to my in-laws I:
_____ feel very comfortable in knowing what to call them
_____ wish I knew what to call them (Mom, Dad, or first name)

I feel that my spouse is:
_____ too close to his/her family
_____ not close enough to his/her family

My spouse feels that I am:
_____ too close to my family
_____ not close enough to my family

I wish:
_____ I felt more comfortable with my spouse's family
_____ my spouse felt more comfortable with my family

My spouse and I disagree over:
_____ how much time to spend with family
_____ whose family to visit for the holidays

I sometimes feel pulled between:
_____ what my family wants from me and what my spouse wants from me
_____ my loyalty to my own family and my loyalty to my spouse's family

Since our wedding, my relationship with my own family:
_____ has changed for the better
_____ has changed for the worse

Since our wedding, my relationship with my spouse's family:
_____ has changed for the better
_____ has changed for the worse

Review the statements that you marked and use them as a springboard for a discussion about your in-laws.

- Do not gloss over any tough spots your mentorees address. Let them know it is okay to talk about struggles.
- Don't forget to talk enthusiastically about the positive points of marriage.
- Use your own true-life stories as a point of encouragement.
- Be vulnerable when appropriate (e.g., letting them know your own struggles).
- Encourage a shift in allegiance from family of origins to their new partnership.
- Be open to learning how you can learn from your newly married couple.
- Go easy with giving advice.
- Empathize with your couple by putting yourself in their shoes.
- Listen, listen, listen.

Note: If you are part of a sponsored marriage mentoring team, do not forget to complete the Seventh-Month Meeting Report (in appendix C of this book) and send it to your marriage mentor coordinator.

> *C*ome to the edge," he said.
> They said, "We are afraid."
> "Come to the edge," he said.
> They came. He pushed them ... and they flew.
> GUILLAUME APOLLINAIRE

CHAPTER SIX:

THE TWELFTH-MONTH MEETING: CELEBRATION

Herbstein, Germany has become somewhat of a mecca for wedding anniversaries. Many years ago, governmental authorities of Herbstein decided that everyone who got married in their town should plant a tree, a sapling birch. Within a year, more than one hundred white-barked birch trees stood along the *Strasse der Ehe*, Marriage Road. And every year, many of the couples who planted the trees return on their anniversaries to see how their saplings have grown.

Wedding anniversaries are so special—especially the first one. For most couples it marks the place where they step out of the rookie role.

THE TWELFTH MONTH OF MARRIAGE

As with the three- and seven-month meetings, this one may bring up a few fairly expected issues for exploration. While not every couple encounters the same issues during their first twelve months, there are some areas that are quite predictable: coping with gender issues, becoming soul mates, and celebration. Being aware of these issues can make you better prepared for your session.

Coping with Gender Issues

The contrasts between women and men are striking, especially after living with the opposite gender for about a year. By virtue of being male and female, married couples think, feel, and behave differently from one another. While there are always exceptions to the rule, research and experience have revealed a fundamental and powerful distinction between the sexes: Men focus on achievement, women focus on relationships. It sounds overly simplistic, and it probably is, but discovering this general rule is part of the first year of marriage. It takes experience to accept the difference. The period of courtship and the early months of marriage hide fundamental differences. But by the time a couple comes to their first anniversary, gender issues emerge.

Becoming Soul Mates

Every couple longs to be soul mates. Most new couples expect marriage to quench their spiritual longings. But developing the deeper spiritual aspect of marriage doesn't often come easily. Some couples in their first year, for example, begin with lofty expectations about how they will cultivate the soul of marriage. They may set aside a quiet time to read the Bible and pray together as a couple, only to find that their behavior doesn't always measure up to their good intentions. Many newlyweds feel guilty for not knowing how to nurture one another's soul.

Celebration

The completion of the first year of marriage is a time of celebration and reflection for newlyweds. While one year may not seem long to you, it is quite an accomplishment for most new couples. And celebrating this passage is something they have looked forward to with eager anticipation.

WHAT TO TALK ABOUT

This session should certainly be initiated with celebration. The first anniversary is a significant milestone and to have a mentor couple join in the celebration can double a young couple's sense of progress. So let them, from the top, know that you celebrate their accomplishment. Your session, however, should not simply be a party. It is a critical point in the mentoring relationship. Early in the session, you may cover any unfinished business from your last meeting. What topics do your mentorees still ponder? What issues need more clarification? What insights have since changed a particular view?

Next, you may want to explore the mentorees' shared-vision goals by reviewing how well they met their various one-year objectives. Highlight the goals they were especially good at meeting and relieve any guilt for goals that have not yet been met. Before leaving this topic you will want to underscore the value of setting goals for their marriage and challenge them to do so again for their next year. In fact, you may want to have them explore their next set of goals with you.

As always, you may give your mentorees an opportunity to bring up topics of interest by inquiring about their reading of *Marriage Partnership* magazine or marriage books they have been reading. Of course, it doesn't hurt to highlight something that was valuable to you and your marriage as well. This kind of modeling can be more powerful than anything else you do.

To bring closure to your year of marriage mentoring, we recommend that you facilitate a review of the mentorees' first year. Ask them about their highlights. Ask them to identify the most important lessons they learned about marriage. What was their biggest challenge? What will they remember most about this first year? You may want to explore what they have acquired as a result of the mentoring relationship. If you are up to it, ask them how you could improve your mentoring skills.

One of the most effective capstones we have discovered for this final session is to read a portion of a poem by Tori Carlstrom Britton called *"Still Married After Just One Year"*:

Our ring-fingered friends said
the first year would be the hardest.
But then again this bride,
with one cake-top sliver still soft
on the second shelf of the refrigerator,
doesn't quite know why either.

And I don't care if we ever figure it out.
I just don't want to forget, that's all.
I don't want you to wipe this first year away
with your infectious appetite for now.
I don't want me to fictionalize it,
rewriting it into gothic romance
or gothic horror,
making lukewarmth out of heat,
or light out of tears,
or nought
from its intricate knottiness.

So let's not.
Even if the days come when,

at your retirement dinner,
you are honored for two-point-five decades of
dedicated, satisfying, and well-paid service,
And even if the day comes when I can juggle daily writing
with daily prayer, Bible, eating, sleeping,
and enhancing the lives of you and our 2.5 children,
accomplishing all without weeping or gnashing of teeth.

Even if those days of comfort
should miraculously arrive, by divine grace,
may I sit more than once again
in the warmth of your sweater
in the curve of this chair
taking captive your latest notebook and new favorite pen
and reminisce about those times in Chapter One
when the only thing we had holding us together
was the love of God
and how it was
enough.

After reading this poem (and perhaps providing them with a copy of it), you may want to pray for your mentorees, giving them a blessing for their future.

A QUICK REVIEW LIST FOR THE THIRD MENTOR MEETING

As always, you may find it helpful to review the following suggestions before your final session:

- Celebrate the anniversary of your mentorees' first year.
- Remember that your primary role is to be a supportive model.
- Review the highlights of the couple's first year and affirm them in their successes.
- Challenge your mentorees to set and pursue goals for the next year of marriage.
- Use stories from your own marriage history to encourage your mentorees.
- Explore the issue of soul-care in marriage by asking your mentorees about how they can nurture each other's spirituality.
- Be open to learning how you can learn from your newly married couple, especially about how you can be more effective mentors.
- As always, go easy with giving advice—and listen with a third ear.

Note: If you are part of a sponsored marriage mentoring team, do not forget to complete the Twelfth-Month Meeting Report and the Marriage Mentoring Year-End Feedback Form (in appendix C of this book) and send it to your marriage mentor coordinator.

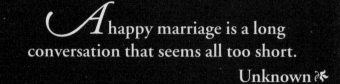

Chapter Seven:

Mentoring Between Meetings

"It was just good to know that somebody was there for us." We have heard this sentiment time and again from couples who have come through a year of marriage mentoring. In one way or another, mentorees express their appreciation, not just for the sessions they spend with their mentors, but for a general sense that another more experienced couple was looking out for them, that they were being cared for even in between their sessions. In fact, we feel that the connection you maintain between meetings is just as important as your sessions together.

A Random Sampling of Ideas

We have worked with literally hundreds of mentor couples and have picked up many creative and clever ideas for making meaningful mentoring connections. In this brief chapter we simply share these ideas to stimulate you to think of ways to shape your own mentoring relationship.

- Keep your couple's name (along with their phone number and address) posted in a convenient location. This will help you keep them in mind, pray for them, and make it easier to send them mail or make a call.

- Mail a note of encouragement to your couple from time to time. Even a brief card saying that you are thinking of them can be a real uplift.

- Send your couple a helpful article about marriage you have read. Simply clip it out, write a quick note on it, and drop it in an envelope to them.

- With the permission of your mentorees, make contact with their parents. Let their parents know of your mentoring relationship and how you enjoy their children.

- Let your couple know about an upcoming marriage seminar or a guest speaker (at your church or a community function).

- Send your couple a few coupons for things they might use. Simply clip coupons for various products over a few days and send them to your couple.

- Invite your couple to your church if they are looking for a new church home.
- Let your couple know about an upcoming television news show that has a segment about marriage.
- Invite your couple into your home for a meal or dessert.
- Send your couple a Christmas card with a personal note about how you will be thinking of them during the holiday season.
- "Allow" your couple to baby-sit your kids. (This is an activity that many newlyweds enjoy as they think about their future family.)
- Send your couple an anniversary card. Do this not just on their first anniversary, but for years that follow. This is a special way of staying in touch. After all, how many anniversary cards do you receive?

This list is certainly not exhaustive. You will develop your own style of mentoring in between meetings. Please let us know about your creative ideas so we might share them with other mentor couples. Write to:

Drs. Les and Leslie Parrott
Center for Relationship Development
Seattle Pacific University
Seattle, WA 98119

> *D*on't do nothing
> just because you can't do everything.
> BOB PIERCE

CHAPTER EIGHT:

WHEN
PROFESSIONAL HELP
IS NEEDED

Most couples have difficult problems from time to time, but some couples have difficult problems most of the time. According to Miriam Arond and Samuel Pauker in *The First Half of Marriage* (Warner Books, 1987), *half* of all newlyweds report having "significant marital problems."

As mentors, be sure to consider the frequency and intensity of the problems your mentorees face. According to research, it is possible to predict that a marriage will be fraught with more and more adjustment problems if the following are true:

- The couple meets or marries shortly after a significant loss (e.g., parent dies).
- The wish to distance from one's family of origin is a factor in the marriage.
- The family backgrounds of each spouse are significantly different (religion, education, social class, ethnicity, and so on).
- The couple resides either extremely close to or at a great distance from either family of origin.
- The couple is overly dependent on either extended family.
- The couple marries before age twenty.
- The couple marries after an acquaintance of less than six months.
- The couple marries after more than three years of engagement.
- The wedding occurs without family or friends present.
- The wife becomes pregnant before or within the first year of marriage.
- Either spouse has a poor relationship with his or her siblings or parents.
- Either spouse considers his or her childhood or adolescence an unhappy time.
- Marital patterns in either family were unstable.

Of course, none of these situations is certain to lead to difficulties, but if your couple faces several of these situations they may be in need of professional help even during their first year.

Couples who do not necessarily face some of the above situations can still benefit from counseling. Newly married couples need to complete a number of tough tasks. Failure to succeed in a number of areas contributes to what researchers have identified as "duration of marriage effect"—the tendency for marital satisfaction to decrease over time. These tasks include the following:

- Establishing marital roles and responsibilities through negotiation and adjusting expectations.
- Providing emotional fulfillment and support for each other by learning how to give and receive love and affection.
- Adjusting personal habits such as sleep patterns, spending behavior, and so on.
- Negotiating gender roles that reflect individual personalities, skills, needs, interests, values, and equity.
- Making sexual adjustments with each other by learning how to physically discover mutual pleasure and satisfaction.
- Establishing family and employment priorities by learning to balance and negotiate.

- Developing effective communication skills that allow resolution to conflicts.
- Managing budgetary and financial matters.
- Establishing relationships with extended family and setting boundaries between their marriage and families of origin.
- Participating in the larger community by making friends with other married couples and being involved in the community.

Each of the above tasks can be given a boost through professional marriage counseling.

If for any reason you suspect the couple you are mentoring needs outside help, gently bring the issue up with your couple. Ask them if they think additional outside help would be beneficial. Remember that any hurting couple will be relieved to know that help is available. In addition, newlyweds that are truly baffled by a spouse are generally open to the help of someone who can help. If your couple is interested in counseling, here are a few sources for finding a competent counselor in their area:

American Association of Christian Counselors	800–5–COUNSEL
Christian Association for Psychological Studies	714–337–5117
Focus on the Family	719–531–3400
Minirth-Meier New Life Clinic	800–332–8336
Rapha Treatment Centers	800–227–2657

CHAPTER NINE:

THE BOOMERANG EFFECT OF MARRIAGE MENTORING

"I don't know how much we helped Doug and Sarah," Joan told us, "but *we* sure got a lot out of it." Joan laughed as she told us about being a marriage mentor couple along with her husband of eighteen years, Larry.

"Helping a young couple seemed to spark a lot of things in our own marriage that we had neglected," Larry added.

Joan and Larry agreed that the benefits of being marriage mentors went both ways—to mentorees, of course, but also to mentors.

The report Joan and Larry were relaying to us has been repeated time and again with the marriage mentors we have observed. Almost mystically, something wonderful happens when a more mature couple reaches out to a new couple. We call it the boomerang effect. By helping another couple form and live out their dreams, one's own dreams for marriage are reawakened and fulfilled.

C. S. Lewis had a friend, Charles Williams, who warned him: "No mind is so good that it does not need another mind to counter and equal it." The same warning is true for marriage mentors. If you will allow the process of mentoring to do good in your own marriage, if you will be receptive to the two-way process, the blessing you find in mentoring will be doubled.

WHAT MENTORING WILL DO FOR YOU

As an effective mentor couple, you will eventually recognize how much you receive from the couple you mentor. Because you have taken the time to be present with a questioning couple, your own "answers" will become clearer. The wisdom of a new bride and groom, perhaps so different from your own, will complement and clarify your own understanding of marriage. You will find that the ones you are mentoring will become, in some ways, *your* teachers, *your* mentors.

You will also be refreshed by this relationship. Mentoring will rejuvenate your marriage with the energy of youth. Almost by osmosis, the vim and vigor for marriage that new couples enjoy will begin to rub off on you.

Simply being around their energetic spirits will revive and rejuvenate your marriage.

And perhaps the most common aspect of the boomerang effect is satisfaction. As mentors, you will enjoy the satisfaction of a job well done. When a married couple successfully works on any project together—wallpapering a room, raking autumn leaves, and so on—there is a sense of satisfaction that results. And when a couple works on a project that has lasting value, even eternal significance—such as marriage mentoring—there is an overwhelming sense of having done good!

The diversity of marriage mentoring styles and the complexity of newly married couples prevent a detailed listing of exactly how your mentoring experience will be mutually beneficial. But we know that it will.

In Norman Russell's *The Lives of the Desert Fathers*, there is a story about an ascetic who lived alone in the desert. But eventually he returned to the life of community after a dream in which an angel advised him: "The brethren to whom you gave spiritual counsel will come to console you, and they will bring you gifts. Welcome them, eat with them, and always give thanks to God for them."

As marriage mentors, one of the most important aspects of your mentoring is the awareness that your mentorees bring you gifts and that you need to welcome them, eat with them, and always give thanks to God for them.

OUR PRAYER FOR YOU

In the *Odyssey*, the hero, Odysseus, had an elderly friend and adviser named Mentor. Before Odysseus went to fight in the Trojan War, he made Mentor the guardian of his son, Telemachus. And in a very real sense you will become the guardians of the marriages you mentor.

So our prayer for you is that your mentorees would dare to speak of their joys and sorrows, entrusting you with their hearts, and that in return you would guard their marriage as you rely on God's strength and grace to guard yours.

APPENDIX A

RESOURCES FOR NEWLYWEDS (AND "OLDYWEDS")

There are dozens and dozens of helpful resources for newlyweds and marriage mentors. The following list is not exhaustive, but it offers reading you and your mentoree couple might find of interest.

Augsburger, David. *Sustaining Love: Healing and Growth in the Passages of Marriage*. Ventura, CA.: Regal Books, 1988.

This book addresses four central decades of change which occur as couples mature in marriage: the dream of the twenties, the disillusionment of the thirties, the discovery of the forties, and the depth of the fifties.

Conway, Jim and Sally Conway. *Traits of a Lasting Marriage: What Strong Marriages Have in Common*. Downers Grove, ILl.: InterVarsity Press, 1991.

Jim and Sally Conway surveyed 186 couples to discover what makes a good marriage work. From that survey, along with the insights gained from over thirty-five years of marriage and counseling, they identified ten key traits.

Crabb, Larry. *Men and Women: Enjoying the Difference*. Grand Rapids: Zondervan, 1991.

Men and women, says Dr. Crabb, share a deadly problem—we are committed, first of all, to ourselves. But Crabb shows the way for men and women to understand each other and experience deep enjoyment of our differences.

Dobson, James. *Love for a Lifetime: Building a Marriage That Will Go the Distance*. Portland, OR: Multnomah Press, 1987.

This book is especially for single adults, engaged couples, and husbands and wives who have not yet reached their tenth anniversaries. It focuses on the principles and concepts that will help armor-plate a marriage and equip it to "go the distance."

Driscoll, R. *The Binds That Tie: Overcoming Standoffs and Stalemates in Love Relationships*. Lexington: Lexington Books, 1991.

In this insightful book, Dr. Richard Driscoll shows how to overcome destructive patterns that cause our marital relationships to become stagnant. He explains why troublesome patterns seem to carry us along in spite of our wishes for change and provides the tools to establish positive and fulfilling relationship patterns.

Farrel, Bill and Pam, Jim and Sally Conway, *Pure Pleasure: Making Your Marriage a Great Affair*. Downers Grove, IL: InterVarsity, 1994.

In this book you will meet real couples who discover real ways to deal with sexual issues in their marriages. They steer newlywed couples away from negative patterns and discuss such challenges a:restoring passion in your marriage and talking in a way that leads to intimacy.

Harley, Willard, F. Jr. *His Needs, Her Needs: Building an Affair-proof Marriage*. Grand Rapids: Revell, 1986.

This popular book shows couples how identifying and meeting the most important needs of each other will deepen the love and desire they have for each other. It is a book written to educate couples on how to sustain romance, increase intimacy, and deepen awareness year after year.

Hendrix, Harville. *Getting the Love You Want: A Guide for Couples*. New York: Henry Holt & Co., 1988.

Dr. Harville Hendrix, a marriage therapist and pastoral counselor, has discovered how to defuse power struggles. Through the skills he teaches in this guide, a couple can transform their power struggles into a mutually beneficial process of spiritual and emotional growth.

Hybels, Bill and Lynne. *Fit to Be Tied: Making Marriage Last a Lifetime*. Grand Rapids: Zondervan, 1991.

Bill and Lynne Hybels draw from a sound biblical foundation and rich personal experience for this frank book about the heights and depths of marriage. It deals with issues of compatibility and offers help on restoring peace in the midst of turbulence.

Joy, Donald and Robbie. *Lovers: Whatever Happened to Eden?* Waco, TX: Word, 1987.

This books reverently questions the traditional views of sex roles in marriage. Firmly rooted in Scripture, not current trends, the authors challenge the reader to probe theology as well as biological research. They write with warm anecdotes from their own relationship and openly describe their sometimes painful pilgrimage from the traditional marriage model to a relationship as equals.

Lauer, Jeanette, and Lauer, Robert. *No Secrets? How Much Honesty Is Good for Your Marriage?* Grand Rapids: Zondervan, 1993.

This book is rooted in Scripture and filled with stories from the lives of real people who are struggling with perplexing questions about honesty. *No*

Secrets? helps you to be honest without being blunt, to uncover secret expectations that might be hurting your marriage, to face the impact a "harmless lie" can have on your marriage, and to understand what happens when a part of your life is hidden from your spouse.

Markman, Howard, Scott, Stanley and Susan Blumberg. *Fighting for Your Marriage: Positive Steps for Preventing Divorce and Preserving a Lasting Love.* San Francisco: Jossey-Bass, 1994.

This book serves as a manual that will enable couples to discuss difficult issues safely and clearly, use ground rules to resolve conflicts, and enhance fun, friendship, commitment, and spiritual intimacy.

Mason, Mike. *The Mystery of Marriage: As Iron Sharpens Iron.* Portland: Multnomah Press, 1985.

The Mystery of Marriage is a deep meditation on the Christian questions incarnate in the miracle of married love. Mason deals with the earthy realities as well as the profound beauty of love, intimacy, vows, sex, submission, and death.

McManus, Michael. *Marriage Savers: Helping Your Friends and Family Stay Married.* Grand Rapids: Zondervan, 1993.

This book outlines several strategies anyone can use to help a friend or loved one stay married, and offers special help to parents and others who have loved ones working through the difficult early years of marriage.

Olthuis, James. *Keeping Our Troth: Staying in Love Through the Five Stages of Marriage.* San Francisco: Harper & Row, 1986.

Olthuis, drawing from the best in both modern psychotherapy and Christianity, shows how the age-old concept of troth—which implies not only trust in one another, but in God and oneself—provides a strong foundation for marriage.

Pauker, Miriam and Samuel. *The First Year of Marriage: What to Expect, What to Accept, and What You Can Change for a Lasting Relationship.* New York: Warner Books, 1987.

This comprehensive book addresses the tasks of the first year of marriage beginning with the wedding and ending with tools to plan a first anniversary celebration. It offers questionnaires, work-sheets, and checklists to help young couples in identifying and solving problems including conflicts, power struggles, money, families, and communication.

Penner, Clifford and Joyce. *The Gift of Sex.* Waco, TX: Word, 1981.

The Penners have provided an ideal guide for understanding the sexual relationship in marriage with all its pleasure, drive, frustration, and fulfillment. *The Gift of Sex* focuses on the physical dimension, the total experience, moving past sexual barriers, resolving difficulties, and finding help.

Smalley, Gary. *Hidden Keys of a Loving, Lasting Marriage: A Valuable Guide to Knowing, Understanding, and Loving Each Other.* Grand Rapids: Zondervan, 1984.

In this book Gary Smalley helps couples solve some of the most common and persistent problems: how to motivate your spouse to listen to you, how to strengthen affection, and how to be appreciated by your spouse.

Smedes, Lewis. *Caring and Commitment: Learning to Live the Love We Promise.* San Francisco: Harper & Row, 1988.

This insightful and compelling book discusses the risks and rewards of making commitments. Writing in a warm and lively style, Smedes argues eloquently for the importance of choosing freely to make and honor promises.

Snyder, Chuck and Barb. *Incompatibility: Grounds for a Great Marriage.* Sisters, OR: Questar, 1988.

Chuck and Barb Snyder offer frank, helpful, and often hilarious insights about how differences enrich love, decision-making, teamwork, and parenting. They enable couples to learn to truly accept and enjoy one another's personality, realizing that opposites can build a great marriage.

Stevens, Paul. *Marriage Spirituality: Ten Disciplines for Couples Who Love God.* Downers Gove, IL: InterVarsity, 1989.

Paul Stevens presents ten spiritual disciplines for couples to practice together which strengthen both faith and marriage. This book serves as an excellent resource for couples who want to practice their spirituality together.

Stoop, David and Jan. *The Intimacy Factor: How Your Personality and Your Past Affect Your Ability to Love and Be Loved.* Nashville: Thomas Nelson, 1993.

In *The Intimacy Factor,* the Stoops demonstrate how family history, early behavior, birth order, and general home environment all contribute in a profound and critical way to shaping your personality and the way you relate to your spouse. Once you understand these influences, and your different personality types, you will be able to build a more intimate relationship with your spouse.

Wangerin, Walter. *As for Me and My House: Crafting Your Marriage to Last.* Nashville: Thomas Nelson, 1987.

This is a book of rare wisdom, compassion, and honesty regarding the rigorous demands of marriage. Written in his trademark narrative style, Wangerin's book deals with the central tasks of a covenantal marriage relationship at each phase of life.

Wheat, Ed, M.D., and Gloria Perkins. *Love Life for Every Married Couple.* Grand Rapids: Zondervan, 1988.

Physician Ed Wheat identifies the critical issues and offers wise counsel to those who want to build a happier marriage. His work with thousands of couples has led to a focus on improving marriage through sharing, touching, appreciating, and focusing healing attention on your mate.

Worthington, Everett, Jr., and Douglas McMurry. *Marriage Conflicts: A Short-term Structured Model.* Grand Rapids: Baker, 1994.

Marriage Conflicts is practical, strategic counsel for all who are in a helping relationship with couples. In this book the authors discuss how to assess problems, promote confession and forgiveness, help the couple see a new vision for their marriage, and motivate constructive attitudes of valuing one another.

Wright, H. Norman. *The Premarital Counseling Handbook.* Chicago: Moody Press, 1992.

In this excellent volume, marriage expert H. Norman Wright writes for pastors and other premarital counselors. He provides a comprehensive premarital counseling model that addresses family background, personality, roles, expectations, and a wide variety of special issues.

_____ . and Gary Oliver. *How to Change Your Spouse (Without Ruining Your Marriage).* Ann Arbor, MI: Vine Books, 1994.

Norm Wright and Gary Oliver show couples how to start changing each other in positive ways. They cut through manipulation and selfishness and provide insights from over thirty couples who have applied the lessons contained in the book and now enjoy an improved marriage.

_____ . *So You're Getting Married.* Ventura, CA: Regal, 1985.

In this classic book, Norm Wright provides the basis for every life-long happy marriage—total commitment. Along the way he shows engaged couples how to be free form the past, how to control anger and resolve conflicts, how to forgive and pray together, and how to build positive in-law relationships.

_____ . *Communication: Key to Your Marriage.* Ventura, CA: Regal, 1974.

This best-seller teaches couples a dozen methods for reducing friction and conflict, ten ways to handle angry feelings, and ten steps to avoiding anxiety and worry.

_____ . *Holding on to Romance.* Ventura, CA: Regal, 1992.

This one is for every married couple who longs to rekindle the special and sometimes elusive feelings of romance. The author points the way to true romance and reveals why it disappears from time to time—and how you can get it back.

Setting Up
a Mentoring Program

We have a dream: that happily married couples from across the country and around the world will team together and build a network of marriage mentors to support the millions of couples who marry each year. In an effort to make this dream a reality, we have put together a comprehensive kit to help colleges, churches, and other organizations sponsor a marriage preparation program called *Saving Your Marriage Before It Starts*, or SYMBIS for short.

The SYMBIS kit includes:

- *Saving Your Marriage Before It Starts.* This is an engaging book for newlyweds that focuses on seven critically important questions to ask before and after getting married. The questions include: "Can you say what you mean and understand what you hear?" "Have you bridged the gender gap?" And "Do you know how to fight a good fight?"
- *The SYMBIS Workbook for Men.* This is an interactive guide designed especially for men to help them get the most out of reading *Saving Your Marriage Before It Starts.*
- *The SYMBIS Workbook for Women.* This is an interactive guide designed especially for women to help them get the most out of reading *Saving Your Marriage Before It Starts.*
- *The SYMBIS Conflict Card.* This is a tool described in the book that helps couples resolve their differences before their conflicts get the best of them.
- *The SYMBIS Video.* This is an eight-part video series of live sessions with the authors of SYMBIS. It also includes brief can-

did pieces of young couples interacting with the presentation material. These twenty-five minute videos can be used in individual sessions with a couple or in larger venues, such as a classroom. The videos provide practical information for newlyweds, and they model how couples can get the most from the SYMBIS material.

- *The SYMBIS Leader's Guide.* This comprehensive guide provides numerous suggestions for customizing the SYMBIS program to a particular setting. It includes exercises, icebreakers, outlines, and tips for leading informative sessions and for facilitating lively discussions. It also contains detailed information on recruiting and equipping marriage mentors.

- *The Marriage Mentor Manual.* This kit also includes the book you are holding. *The Marriage Mentor Manual* was written to be informative without being wordy. It was also designed to be affordable. This allows an organization to purchase numerous copies of *The Marriage Mentor Manual* and provide them to couples who are volunteering in their program to mentor younger couples. The idea is that a church, for example, would use this SYMBIS kit in preparing couples for marriage and then help coordinate a local team of marriage mentors from the congregation.

The bottom line is that marriage mentoring works. It increases the chances that a young couple will build a love that lasts a lifetime, it spurs mentors to a deeper level of intimacy in their own marriage, and it distributes the work of pastors and professionals who have for too long shouldered this responsibility alone. In short, marriage mentoring is a win-win-win proposition for everyone involved.

For more information on purchasing the SYMBIS curriculum kit, call 1-800-727-3480.

APPENDIX C

REPORT FORMS

If you are using this manual in conjunction with a sponsoring organization, school, or church, the following forms are to be used for keeping your marriage mentor coordinator informed about how things are going. These report forms are critical to the success of this mentoring program, so please help your coordinator by filling them out and returning them.

If you are not a part of a marriage mentorship program, you may still find these report forms helpful. You might use them as a way of tracking your mentorship meetings and recording your observations for future reference.

Third-Month Meeting Report

Your Names: Phone

Mentor Couple: Date

Thanks for taking the time to fill this out.

The setting for our contact was:

In general, how is your couple doing?

       Poorly   1   2   3   4   5   6   7   Excellent

Couple's Tough Spots:

Success Stories:

What would help you in the mentoring process?

Seventh-Month Meeting Report

Your Names: Phone

Mentor Couple: Date

Thanks for taking the time to fill this out.

The setting for our contact was:

In general, how is your couple doing?

        Poorly   1   2   3   4   5   6   7   Excellent

Couple's Tough Spots:

Success Stories:

How may we help you in the mentoring process?

Twelfth-Month Meeting Report

Your Names: Phone

Mentor Couple: Date

Thanks for taking the time to fill this out.

The setting for our contact was:

In general, how is your couple doing?

Poorly 1 2 3 4 5 6 7 Excellent

Couple's Tough Spots:

Success Stories:

Please return your "Year-end Feedback Form" along with this report. Thanks.

LINCOLN CHRISTIAN COLLEGE AND SEMINARY

Marriage Mentoring Year-End Feedback Report

Please complete this evaluation form shortly after you have completed the mentoring program (i.e., after the anniversary contact). Please be frank in answering the questions and feel free to use additional pages.

Mentor Couple: Date

How would you rate your personal experience as mentors?

Male:
   Not so hot   1   2   3   4   5   6   7   Truly enjoyed it!

Female:
   Not so hot   1   2   3   4   5   6   7   Truly enjoyed it!

How would you rate the effectiveness of the mentoring program as a whole?

   Poorly   1   2   3   4   5   6   7   Excellent

What was the toughest part of mentoring your couple?

What could be done to make mentoring a better experience for you?

What could be done to make it a better experience for the couple you mentored?

What advice would you give to another marriage mentor couple?

Do you think you will stay in touch with your mentor couple?

Would you consider mentoring another couple in the future?
   Yes ❐   No ❐